WONDERFUL
COPENHAGEN

Introduction

Copenhagen's origin is due to three fortunate occurrences. The first was an abundance of herrings. „There were so many fish that one could scoop them up in a bucket." The next was its topography, a natural harbour between Zealand and Amager. The third was its geographical position. From fishing follows trade and the place was handy for buyers from the Baltic lands. For many years the place had no real

name and was simply called „Havn" i.e. port.

„Havn" grew; so fast that the German Hanseatic ports, Bremen, Hamburg, Lubeck and others felt that their interests were threatened and attacked and burned the place down. However, it was built up again and continued to expand.

In 1167, the warrior-bishop Absalon fortified the place by building a castle and the city reckons this date as its foundation. The place was at first called „Købmændenes Havn" (Merchants Port) which soon changed to „København" (Marketport) = Copenhagen.

Absalon's castle was not enough to stave off the attacks. In truth it must also be stated that neither did the Danes hold back. Absalon attacked the towns on the Baltic coasts with large fleets of viking ships and sailed far up the Russian rivers. It was a mixture of crusade, colonisation, trade and trade war.

The Hanseatic League was our strongest anagonist in the race

for trade and influence. Our slender viking ships were fast and they could tack and sail 50 degrees to the wind. The „Cog", the ship preferred by the Hanseatic League, was slow and unsuitable for tacking, but could carry a larger cargo with a much smaller crew. Already at that time they were aware of the influence of wages on the end result.

Meanwhile Copenhagen grew in importance and was surrounded by fortified walls and ramparts. The city's emblem was Three Towers. In 1343 King Valdemar Atterdag made it the capital city of the kingdom. There came a new time of prosperity for the city which prompted the usual reaction from the Hanseatic League; in 1368 Copenhagen was demolished - and built up again.

Christian IV reigned from 1588 to 1648. He was - and remained - a legend. A colourful and enterprising king. He sailed to North Cape in Norway to affirm Denmark's rights there. In Iceland he established a trade monopoly which especially hit the Hanseatic ports. He sent a fleet to India where he acquired Tranquebar. He reinforced the Danish army and navy; started up Danish industry; strengthened Copenhagen's fortifications and enhanced the city with many beautiful buildings.
He was an ambitious and warlike king. He lost most of the wars, often let down by his allies. At his death the kingdom was split and impoverished. However, Copenhagen was more beautiful than ever before.

In 1658 a Swedish army of 6,000 men approached the city. It was led by one of the most able commanders of the time, Carl X Gustav. There was great consternation in the city, but when the king, Frederik III, declared that he would not flee, but fight and risk „*dying in his nest*", the courage and morale of the citizens was greatly strengthened.

The whole city worked to improve the fortifications. Houses outside the ramparts were evacuated and burned down to give a free firing line. In February 1659 the Swedes stormed the city, but the attack was beaten off. We had only 3,000 soldiers, but also the civil guard, sailors and 1,200 students, artisans and other volunteers manned the ramparts. The Swedes had 580 fallen while the Danish losses were 12!

In gratitude for the city's efforts, the king issued a letter of privilege which gave the citizens the right to be consulted in the city's affairs. The city was also awarded a new coat of arms: still the Three Towers - but now encircled by flags, lions and weaponry (page 83).

In the next century and a half the city was spared attack, but not fire. In 1728 a fire raged which demolished 2/5 of the city. A new fire in 1795 and the British bombardment in 1807 caused great destruction. Therefore the city has very few houses left from the Middle Ages.

Practical information
Please note that in the text it is stated which train station is closest to each of the attractions - and that on page 2 there is a map with information about DSB (Danish State Railway) traffic services in the city and environs.

The Copenhageners

It is said, that people living in ports are more friendly than others. In Madrid, if you ask a policeman the way, you will get an answer, but it will be quite clear that he has other tasks. In Copenhagen, a policeman, if he does not actually take you to the place requested, will with pleasure go along a little way in order to point it out. A chance passerby will also be interested in your problems.

In traffic, Copenhageners are not nearly as amusing as they are in Madrid or Rome. There, if you signal that you have got into the wrong lane, you see them grinning in the other car, and they hold back for you. That seldom happens here.

Be careful of cyclists. If you indicate to the right when driving in a car, look carefully behind you. A cyclist continuing forward will keep to his course and speed trusting implicitly that the highway code will be adherred to, even though you are indicating and maybe already have started to turn.

We are bound by rules, and foreigners smile at people who stand waiting for the green light at a pedestrian crossing - even though there is not a vehicle in sight. That would not happen in Paris or New York.

Watch out also for the sausage stand men. When they close, they trundle off with their whole business. It is a tacit Copenhagen agreement that they have right of way.

The Fortress

1856. Like a fortress, Copenhagen lies surrounded by ramparts. Bridges straddle the moat. The gates are shut at night. It is safe behind the ramparts. The bourgeoisie enjoy life. A perfect idyl - but with problems: there are far too many people in too small a space. Many live in miserable hovels. Something has to be done. There are hectic discussions: should the ramparts be removed? This came about, but not until 1872. Then things started to happen. The city, so to speak, exploded.

Speculative builders were eager to build in every direction. Luckily, the City Council ensured that parts of the fortifications were preserved for the public good - some as green spaces: Østre Anlæg, the Botanical Gardens, Ørsted Park and Tivoli. The beautiful lake in Tivoli is part of the original moat.
Then came buildings. Find „Frihedsstøtten" (Pillar of Freedom) up on the right hand side in the plate above. It is out in the country. Compare with its

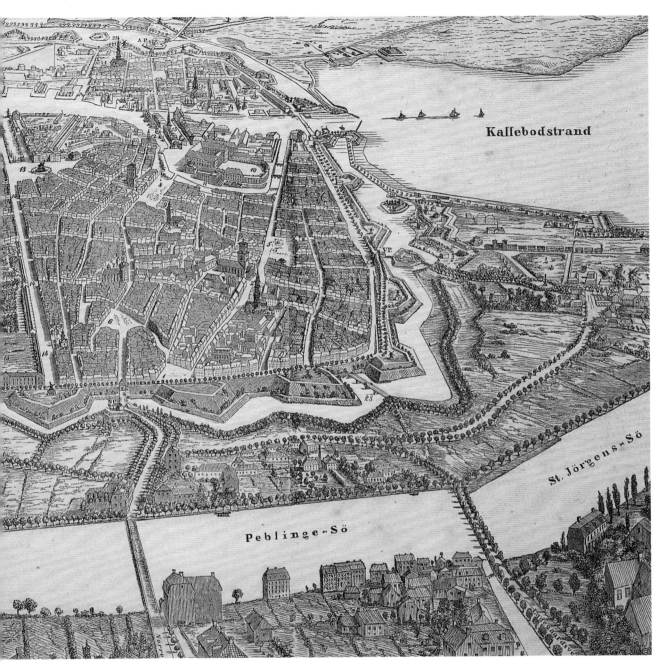

Kallebodstrand

St. Jörgens-Sö

Peblinge-Sö

surroundings today in the little photo underneath. There is only about 100 years between the two pictures.

The plate here gives a good impression of how modern Copenhagen is influenced by the past. The City, with its narrow streets, castles and large churches lies compactly behind the now demolished ramparts. Everything on the other side is the „new town". One understands why the railway stations are named „Østerport" (Eastgate), „Nørreport" (Northgate) and „Vesterport" (Westgate).

In 1915 „Boulevardbanen" (the Boulevard line) was laid out in the old terrain which prudently had been excluded from the building-boom after the removal of the ramparts. Today it is DSB's railway, the network that binds the city and surrounding area together, together with the Coast railway, the connection with Helsingør and further to Sweden and Norway, which run in what used to be the city moat.

Everything which can be seen on the other side of the railway cutting is „the new town" which arose after 1872. It stretches for miles and never really ends. Highrise buildings give way to houses: between Copenhagen and Helsingør, 40 km to the north, one rides through a continuous unbroken urban area.

In a few places there are still visible remains of the fortifications. Jarmers Tower is a remnant of the late Middle Age fortress and the ruin stands where „Vester Voldgade" West Rampart Street meets „Nørre Voldgade" North Rampart Street.

„Kastellet" (The Citadel) raised by Christian IV in 1616 - still stands as a fortress. The gates are manned by soldiers and the place has that rugged stamp that fits a fortification. One need not be intimidated, but can safely pass the guard, go inside, take in the atmosphere and visit the lovely church which was consecrated in 1704.

On the evening of Great Prayer Day, the Student Choral Association sings in the church. The church is completely full. After the concert everybody leaves, escorted by soldiers with pipes and drums, beating the tattoo on the ramparts. Later, according to an old tradition, people promenade on the ramparts.

In the area Christianshavn - Christiansharbour - the layout is also the same as in former times. Behind the rampart one can see The Church of Our Saviour with its strange outside stairway leading to the top of the tower - and a wonderful view over the city.

(DSB: København H)

13

The monarchy

The Danish royal family has lived in the palace of Amalienborg in Copenhagen since 1794 - at least for most of the year. The majority of people in Copenhagen consider the royal family to be fellow citizens and the present queen has on several occasions stated that she considers herself as a Copenhagener.

The palace complex was not originally intended to be the royal residence. The eight-sided square with the four palaces and the round church crowned with a dome - Frederiks Church, also called the Marble Church, which is the centre-piece, was built for families of the nobility. It was almost certainly inspired by the then Place Louis XV, now the Place de la Concorde in Paris. The royal family moved in after the huge Christiansborg Palace on Slotsholmen burned down in 1794.

Amalienborg Palace is guarded by the Royal Life Guards, but otherwise is open to both motor traffic and pedestrians.

The Danish monarchy is the eldest in Europe. It has existed in a direct line since the middle of the 10th century, which is more than 1,000 years.

(DSB: Østerport)

Margrethe II & Prince Consort Henrik

Crown Prince Frederik of Denmark

Prince Joachim of Denmark

In Denmark, Copenhagen is often called King's Copenhagen, and the concept „King" has also included a reigning queen since a change in the Constitution and Law of Succession in 1953.

Ever since Denmark's first free constitution in 1849, the form of government has been constitutional monarchy - that is to say that the reigning monarchs powers in making laws and the exercise of government are purely formal.

It is often debated whether this form of government can be justified according to modern, parliamentary-democratic principles. Critics have especially emphasised the risk of political, maybe even military pressure on the monarchy in extreme situations. In practice, as long as Denmark has had a democratic form of government, there has very seldom been any disagreement between the monarch and the democratically based institutions, the Parliament and the Government.

The Royal Life Guards was founded in 1658. The bearskin busby and the cartridge pouch belong among the best known details in the history of military uniforms. The Life Guards are an infantry regiment and most of the soldiers have volunteered to do their military service there. The regiment's most important right and duty is to protect the royal family.

The Changing of the Guard - a big attraction for both the people of Copenhagen and tourists - takes place on Amalienborg Palace every day at 12 p.m. and the guards march from and to their barracks at Rosenborg Castle. The march through the city lasts about 1/2 an hour by different routes. The Guard's band accompanies only when the Queen is in residence at Amalienborg.

On the personal level, the Queen has developed to become an active artist with a reputation as a personality in cultural activities. She has promoted a lively dialogue with the population and expressed values and opinions that to a great extent unite the nation.

Her double role as head of state and artist has compelled deep respect and strengthened the special devotion that Danes feel for their monarch. Some examples of her artistic work:

Illustration of the British author John R. Tolkiens „Lord of the Rings".

Margrethe Alexandrine Thorhildur Ingrid was only 31 years old when her father, Frederik IX , died in 1972 and it became her task to carry on the tradition as head of state. A task that seems overwhelming - there is no job description for a reigning queen in a constitutional monarchy.

Translation into Danish - in collaboration with the Prince Consort - of the French authoress Simone de Beauvoir's novel „Tous les hommes sont mortels". (Under the penname H.M. Vejerberg (weigher-mountain) i.e. a danisation of Prince Henrik's family name, Montpezat).

A large number of pictorial works and important scenographic commissions.

Also chasubles, here for Haderslev Cathedral.

It is usual that queens are present at official inaugurations, openings of exhibitions, etc. Our Queen also attends, but is often seen far from „the polished floors". Here she is in overalls after a visit to the tunnel construction work under the Great Belt.

Fredensborg Palace by Esrom Lake was ready for occupation in 1722. It was a square building with a huge dome which forms the heart of the present castle which has later been expanded. It is the Royal Family's official residence for part of the Summer.

In the Summer, except in the period of residence, the private apartments are open to the public, with impressive interiors dating from the 18th century. Parts of the large, beautiful park are open to the public all the year round.

The Queen also has a Summer residence in Jutland, at Marselisborg Castle near Århus. One more also: the royal yacht Dannebrog. The Royal Family uses the yacht to visit towns in Denmark and also when on journeys to Greenland and the Farøe Islands.

(DSB: Fredensborg)

The Harbour Front

Copenhagen's harbour is visited by about 20,000 vessels a year, many of which are ferries. Latterly, Copenhagen has become a favourite port of call for cruise ships: in 1988 there were only 75, but now more than 200 arrive annually. The 100 year old Frihavn (free port) has been moved north to a more modern installation as it had become outdated. For several years the old jetties were abandoned, the warehouses deteriorated and were a disgrace to the area, but at the start of the 90s, a new initiative was taken.

(DSB: Østerport)

The warehouses are being renovated and converted to offices. The East Asiatic Company - EAC - has built its new Corporate Center on the central jetty. PFA-Build, a subsidiary company of PFA Pension has built 125 dwellings on the central jetty and India Quay, where the inhabitants have a exceptional chance to live close to the city and yet by the water. Low level mooring places have been made in the quay where a boat can lay to. It is a unique milieu in attractive surroundings with a view of Langelinie and with the yacht harbour and the Citadel nearby. Further on in the harbour, behind the royal yacht, can be seen the headquarters of the Shipping Company A.P.Moller.

A tour along Langelinie (the Longline) - Summer or Winter - is an experience. One gets most out of it on foot. The walk begins on Esplanaden, just beyond Frihedsmuseet (the Liberty Museum) beside Anders Bundgaards impressive Gefion Fountain. The legend tells that the goddess, Gefion, changed her sons into oxen and with them ploughed Zealand out of Sweden's earth. (Naturally there was a deep hole left in Sweden, a lake, and it is correct that Vänern, seen from the air, resembles Zealand.) A little further on one comes to the water. Here lies Langelinie Pavillion where there is a restaurant, and on the top floor the premises of the Royal Danish Yacht Club. If you continue - and one should - you come to the yacht harbour and to Langelinie's actual quay. Here you can see the monument for the Danish

expedition to the east coast of Greenland 1906-8. It was led by Mylius-Erichsen who perished with two companions in 1907.

Immediately afterwards, one comes upon the Little Mermaid. Created by sculptor Edvard Eriksen. Endowed by the Carlsberg brewer and patron of the arts - Carl Jacobsen. Raised in 1913.
„Is it really so small?"
say many people. All in all, many have said much about the Mermaid. She is loved. An object of adoration - sailors believe that it gives luck on a voyage to have touched her. She is hated. She has been covered in paint - even beheaded.

Many people stand or sit for a while by the Mermaid. Maybe they are reflecting on H.C. Andersen's poetic but gruesome fairy tale which was the inspiration for the statue. There is a book available - The Little Mermaid. Her story - The Writer and The Fairy Tale.

Big or small: it is maybe the most famous statue in the world. The Statue of Liberty in New York may be just as well known, but is not the Mermaid prettier?

Big cruise ships lie berthed here during the Summer and the place is alive with cheerful

activity. It can pay to continue right out to the jetty as it is said that here you can buy the best ice cream in town.

Another way of experiencing Langelinie, Copenhagen's harbour and the various canals is by taking a canal tour. There are several companies and different routes. The boats depart from several places in the city centre. The picture shows one at Gammel Strand, near the equestrian statue of Absalon.
One can also embark and land outside the city centre; for example walk out to Langelinie and sail back again.

Shopping

The longest pedestrian street in Europe lies in Copenhagen. It stretches from Rådhuspladsen (City Hall Square) over Gammel Torv, (Old Market Square) Amagertorv and Bremerholm to Kongens Nytorv (Kings New Market Square). We call it „Strøget" and here you can find everything from the old-fashioned clockmaker to a large, modern department store.

However, do not forget your surroundings. Stop for a moment at Gammel Torv. The Caritas fountain was donated by Christian IV in 1608 and at that time was part of Copenhagen's water supply. The city's inhabitants fetched water here which was led from Emdrup Lake through hollowed out tree trunks - a distance of not less than 6 km.

Further along the pedestrian street at Amagertorv No.6 is one of the oldest properties in the city. A merchant's premises from 1616 in Dutch renaissance style.

(DSB: Nørreport)

cafés, cabinet makers, leather shops and much more besides. The choice is maybe not so great as in the department stores, but here one can find specialists who live and breathe for their wares. It is here that one gets specialist advice.

For instance, do not go to a little butcher and ask for salami. Ask instead which of the many types he can reccommend - and remember that in Denmark there is no tradition for bargaining the price.

Near Vesterport station lies the New Scala. Here are restaurants, fashion shops, cinemas, gambling halls, a discotheque and much more, gathered into one impressive building. On the top there is an outdoor cafe with a fine view.

Copenhagen has four large department stores: Magasin, Illum, Daells and Illums Bolighus. They all lie on or near Strøget, the pedestrian street. Here can be found everything the eager buyer's heart desires.

A walk along Strøget's side streets is quite another experience. Here can be found antique shops, butchers, secondhand shops, small charming

(DSB: Nørreport)

Georg Jensen (1866-1935 was a qualified goldsmith and also graduated from the Acadamy of Fine Arts as a sculptor. He managed to combine art and handicraft and to work with material on its own premises.

His motto „*Don't follow the stream, but follow the times if you want to keep young in the struggle*" can be seen as a common denominator in much of his work.

With regard to cutlery, Georg Jensen was a pioneer with his principle that these „*jewels of the table*" deserved just as much care in design and manufacture as a craftsmith's usual work.

The unique design and simple operation has made Bang & Olufsen world famous for their TV and HiFi products. The company's basic principle is the creation of new techniques and design with the highest possible quality. They are represented in the Museum of Modern Art (New York).

Flora Danica was a botanical picture representation covering all known Danish plants. Frederik VI ordered a service from the Royal Porcelain Factory decorated with motives from the work. It was intended for Jekatarina II of Russia, who died in 1796 before the work was completed. By then 1,802 pieces had been produced, and they are today kept in Rosenborg Castle. The service is still produced by Royal Copenhagen Porcelain. It is rather expensive.

The Royal Porcelain Factory was founded in 1775.

At Royal Copenhagen Porcelain in Copenhagen, the sets of Flora Danica, blue fluted and other designs are all hand painted. In the picture one can see that no modern aids are taken into use for this process.

The so-called „Mussel" pattern - the blue fluted design - was introduced at the Royal Porcelain factory in the 18th century. The motives of stylised blue flowers are painted on either porcelain or faience.

Holmegaards Glass Works has existed since 1825 and was established by Countess Danneskiold-Samsøe. The glass works has produced ordinary bottles, crystal glass and finer glass artwork. Here is pictured a „pinchbottle" which is used for snaps.

Fritz Hansen has produced furniture for both Danish and foreign designers. Among the classics should be mentioned: Arne Jacobsen's chairs, „the Ant" and „the Egg" and Piet Hein's „Super Elliptic Table"

On 1st July 1644, Christian IV lost most of one eye in a sea battle which both formally and in practice he led as Chief Admiral. The enemy was the Swedes. In modern Scandinavian naval war records the battle is considered to have been undecided. But the king's words after his injury - „Yet I am still alive" - remain in Denmark's history as a testament that this renaissance king was „The King of the Navy". He loved the navy, and the navy - most probably - also loved him. Already in 1594 a dying Chancellor gave the young inexperienced king a golden rule for his regency. „The fate of Denmark lies on the sea".

Christian IV's reign ended in 1648. He died on 28th February at Rosenborg in Copenhagen and his favourite daughter among his 22 registered children closed his one eye - it was the right one.

Christian IV left his kingdoms and countries split and poverty ridden. Nonetheless, he is probably the king in the whole of Denmark's history who was most beloved by the people. Part of the explanation can be that he was the navy's king. Another reason can be that most of the characteristic buildings in the centre of Copenhagen which are admired by both Danes and foreign guests are, in fact, thought up by Christian IV and built with the king as an exacting supervisor of the architect and as an

The Font in Holmens Church

entrepeneur who inspected every bucket of mortar.

Christian IV's building projects were influenced by Dutch Renaissance style - and by Christian IV. Rosenborg (Rose Castle - on the opposite page) was his „summerhouse". Today it houses the Danish Kings Chronological Collection - a world famous and unique collection which contains the Danish crown jewels. The crown shown here is one of them.

The Stock Exchange was built in 1619-23. The fantastic entwined dragonstails were added in the years immediately afterwards, probably as one of the king's impulses.

(DSB: Nørreport)

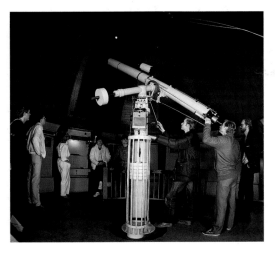

Rundetaarn - The Round Tower - was built on Christian IV's initiative. The foundation stone was laid 7th July 1637. The tower was a part of the Trinitatis complex which was to unite the three most important facilities for 17th century learning: an astronomical observatory, students church and university library.

At the top of the facade is a gilded inscription, a riddle. The sketch for it in Christian IV's own handwriting is kept in the Public Records Office. The riddle can be interpreted in this way: God guide the right wisdom and justice into the heart of the crowned King Christian IV, 1642. 1642 is the year the Round Tower was completed. The Tower's spiral walkway is unique in European architecture. The 209 metre long spiral winds 7 1/2 times around the tower's hollow core and is the only connection between the separate parts of the building.

Through the years, the Round Tower has had many prominent guests. First and foremost one recalls the visit by the Russian Tsar, Peter the Great in 1716. He made the ascent on horseback and his consort was driven up in a horse carriage. The Round Tower has always been popular, and in the 1840s, the humorist Fritz Jürgensen used it as a backdrop for a more macabre story. The text reads „*My god! did you hurt yourself?*"

The library room above Trinity Church's vaults was used as the University library in the years 1657-1861. In 1987 the hall was re-opened after a thorough restoration and the 900 m² room is now used to house changing exhibitions of art, culture, history and science. Today, many classical music concerts are held in the exhibition room.

From the viewing platform 106 feet over street level, the visitor has a fantastic view over old Copenhagen. The platform is fenced by a fine wroughtiron balustrade made by the court art metal smith Kaspar Fincke in 1643. In the railing can be seen Christian IV's monogram and the letters RFP which stand for the king's motto:

Regna Firmat Pietas - Piety strengthens the kingdoms.

The Round Tower is Europe's eldest observatory which is still functional. It was used by the University of Copenhagen until 1861, but today anyone may observe the night sky during the winter half year through the Round Tower's fine astronomical telescope.

With all it has to offer, Christian IV's beautiful and distinctive building is a vital part of Copenhagens cultural milieu.

Jesper Vang Hansen, Rundetaarn

For long periods Christian IV had great need of his seamen. He had tried conditions at sea for himself - although not as an ordinary seaman - and Copenhagen still bears the imprint of his solicitude for „Holmens permanent staff" which the regular members of the navy have been called for centuries.

The Nyboder (new dwellings) quarter at Østerbro (Eastbridge) were built to Christian IV's plan in 1631-48 as free residences for the sailors of the navy. It was devised and constructed as terrace houses, maybe the very first in Europe, but at least the first in Copenhagen.

In 1648 there were 20 rows of one storey buildings containing about 600 family houses. By the standard of the time the dwellings were roomy, light and attractive. Today most people would find them very cramped. But they are attractive.

Today there is only one wing with a single storey and the original dimensions. It is St.Pauls Street 20-40, top left on this page, in the middle of the picture.

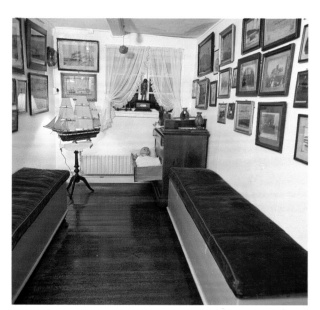

↖(DSB: Østerport) ↑(DSB: København H)

In the centuries after Christian IV, the Nyboder quarter has been regulated and rebuilt many times. Except for St. Pauls Street 20-40, the old terraces have been heightened by one storey. Other houses in the quarter are in no way „real" Nyboder dwellings. A small museum has been established in St. Pauls Street - „Nyboders Memorial Rooms".

The Christianshavn quarter was laid out by Christian IV on the most northern part of the island Amager and some small islands. Originally the purpose was purely defensive.

Like nearly everthing else which Christian IV realised in town planning and buildings, Christianshavn is unmistakably influenced by Holland. Here are canals and there are trees planted along the canals. There are also buildings in the same style as can be seen in Amsterdam.

FREDERIKSBORG

Frederiksborg Castle lies 35 km north of Copenhagen in Hillerød. The oldest part of the castle - the low wings on the left in the picture - were built by Frederik II at the close of the 16th century. In 1600, his son, Christian IV started the work on a new building.

It was completed in 1620 and consists of three wings. In the middle, the royal wing, on the left the west wing with the church and banqueting hall and on the right to the east, the princess wing. There is also the audience chamber with a covered bridge, the secret passage, connecting it to the royal wing.

Until Fredensborg Palace was completed in 1772, Frederiksborg was one of the king's main residences. It was not until the middle of the last century that it again was taken into use by Frederik VII. It is told that the King loved to sit in a window and fish from the lake.

On the night of 17th December 1859, fire broke out in the castle. A westerly storm caused the fire to spread and the next morning the Royal wing, princess wing and the banqueting hall in the church wing were in ruins. Only the black walls were left standing.

It was a national catastrophe. Money was collected over the whole country, and in 1865 the outside of the castle had been rebuilt. Some years later, the brewer, J.C. Jacobsen,

suggested that the castle be utilised as a museum for Denmark's history and offered economic help.

In 1885 The National Historical Museum of Frederiksborg was opened to the public. Today, the museum displays in chronological order people and events from the history of the country in historically correct interiors, a form of museum which has aroused international interest.

(DSB: Hillerød)

SHAKESPEARE

- chose Kronborg for Hamlet, which was no coincidence. The castle, with its appearance, position and fortifications, was unique in Europe.

The function of Kronborg was to guard the entrance to Øresund (The Sound) and be the power base for the collection of Sound Dues. All passing ships were subject to customs. The principal was genial. The captain must declare the worth of his cargo; but the King had the right to buy the cargo for that amount. One needed to guard against declaring too small an amount. The Øresund dues were a very important source of income right up to 1857!

In 1629 fire broke out in the castle and except for the chapel, the whole of the interior was destroyed. Christian IV's rebuilding in 1638 restored to the castle it's former majesty.

Today the castle is a museum. However, there are still cannons on the bastions. A salute is fired from the battery when the royal yacht sails past.

Kronborg has a firm place in the hearts of the Danish people. When one has „Kronborg to starboard" after a visit abroad - one has come home again.

Before & Now

In the water colour by H.G.F. Holm (ca. 1840) one can see from the top of the Round Tower out over the Copenhagen that once lay behind the ramparts. Compared with the picture on the next page, of the same view 100 years later, one can see that not much has changed in the old part of the city. The highrise buildings in the distance stand in the new area, on the other side of the boundary created by the now vanished ramparts.

The fact that high rise buildings are not found in the old part of the city is due not only to respect, but also that a large part of the original city was built on filled in marshland; quite simply, the ground here cannot bear skyscrapers.

It is different in the „new city" which sprang up after the demolition of the ramparts.

Even though it is not noticeable here, there has been some new building in the old city. Some of it is beautiful, but much is, although functional, of such a character that many people today are grieved and think wistfully of the beautiful old rows of houses which were sacrificed.

The pillar of freedom, raised as a memorial to the „abolition of villeinage" - a reform that gave Danish peasants greater freedom - stood outside the city and looked most impressive. Now it has the SAS Royal Hotel with its 20 floors as neighbour.

Thereafter Vesterbrogade (West Bridge Street) continues past it, several kilometres long, and with extensive business premises and dwellings to both sides, Vesterbro (the West Bridge quarter).

The City Hall

The City Hall stands like a proud castle in the city, though there is no portcullis to be forced. The doors are open and during opening hours, anyone is welcome to go inside. One can either look around on one's own or decide to go on a guided tour. There is plenty to see.

The City Hall stood completed in 1905 created by architect Martin Nyrop. It is built in a nordic, vigorous, national romantic variant of Jugend style.

The largest room in the building is the main hall which is used as a polling station at elections, but also for large official occasions, concerts and exhibitions. Here, as everywhere, interesting and often amusing details can be found. There are many rooms and halls - a wedding hall is deco-

rated by Joachim Skovgaard and of course there is the City Council's premises.

The Copenhagen City Council, in principal, still builds on the letter of privilege awarded the city by Frederik III in recognition of the citizens heroic efforts under the Swedish attack in 1659.

It is perpetrated by a 55 member elected municipal council and a so-called municipal corporation - Magistrat - which consists of 7 mayors elected by the municipal council.

A visit can be terminated by a climb to the top of the tower and/or a look into the room with Jens Olsen's world clock, a masterpiece of the clockmakers art.

MARTIN NYROP

Denmark is governed from Christiansborg Palace. The three authorities demanded by the constitution are gathered together in the complex on „Slotsholmen".

The executive power - the Queen (+ government)
The legislative power - Folketinget (Parliament)
The legal power - Højesteret (Supreme Court)

The division between the three powers are written in Latin on Christiansborg's foundation stone and the inscription, in all its impressive Latin simplicity, reads REX, LEX, JUS.

On the square in front of the castle stands a statue of Frederik VII „The Giver of the Constitution". Before the „gift" was given, a revolution broke out, called the March Revolution of 1849. It was, however, very Danish and completely bloodless: a deputation went to the King and on 5th June 1849 an elected parliament moved into the royal castle, Christiansborg.

carriage escorted by Hussar Guards while a detachment of the Life Guards form a guard of honour at the gates. The reception takes place in the Throne Room, but the Queen does not sit down on the throne. This is symbolic: the throne belonged to the kings of the absolute monarchy. By receiving her guests standing up, the Queen makes the point that our monarchy is now constitutional.

On the ceiling there is a painting by Kræsten Iversen: Dannebrog (the Danish flag) falls down from heaven at the battle of Lyndanis in 1219.

The Royal Family lives at Amalienborg, but the Queen receives ambassadors, holds audiences, evening parties for state visits and other festive occasions in the Royal Reception Rooms at Christiansborg. Also the Queen meets with the government in the Council Room to approve draft bills.

When a foreign ambassador is received by the Queen, he arrives in a horse-drawn

Laurits Tuxens large painting: Christian IX and his family at Fredensborg Palace 1886 - is especially interesting. The King was called Europe's father-in-law and the 32 people in the family are from so many different countries that the painting is of interest to a very wide circle.

The richly decorated stucco ceiling in the Queens Library has relief portraits of, amongst others, H.C. Andersen and Grundtvig.

The palace is built on the site where Absalon raised his fortress around 800 years ago, and one can still see its well preserved ruins underneath the building. The castle that stands there today is the third Christiansborg. The two former burned down, but the riding ground and Royal Stables are from the first. The castle chapel is from the second Christiansborg.

The lungs of the city

Because of the short northern summers, Copenhageners use every opportunity to enjoy a sunbeam in the city's many parks.
The Botanical Gardens were laid out in 1874 on part of the old rampart territory. The undulating terrain and the impressive glasshouse make the framework for a wonderful show of rare plants from all over the world.

Frederiksberg castle stands on Valby hill. It was built for Frederik IV in 1699-1703 and today houses the army's officer academy. Frederiksberg garden was laid out adjacent to the castle. A row on the park's canals with views of the small pavillions - the Chinese house, the Swiss chalet and the pretty wooden bridge decorated with parasols - is a fascinating experience.

←(DSB: Nørrreport)   ↓(DSB: Frederiksberg)

The Zoological Gardens, which is neighbour to the castle and its park, is one of the eldest in the world. From the 133 feet tall tower, built in 1905, you can see over the whole of Copenhagen and the Sound to the Swedish coast.

A true Copenhagener would not dream of moving out of town, but on the other hand, enjoys a weekend in a garden. At the turn of the century the first allotments appeared. Areas on the outskirts of the city were divided up into small parcels, allotment gardens. The houses and gardens are tiny, but decorated and well-kept as though they were palaces with great parks. Space is the only limitation for the number of fountains, rows of potatoes and flower arrangements.

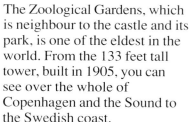

(DSB: Frederiksberg)

Charlottenlund

Wherever one finds oneself in Denmark, it is near the sea. The Danes have an inherited pleasure of being by the sea. On a warm Summer's day Copenhageners stream out of the city. Beaches such as Charlottenlund and Bellevue are the favourites on such days.

The Danes have a tradition for sailing, formerly only of necessity, but now also for enjoyment and the sake of sport. This has resulted in Olympic gold medals in several boat classes and boat designers with international reputations. Prince Henrik is an enthusiastic sailor in the Dragon class.

Bellevue

↑(DSB: Charlottenlund)   →(DSB: Klampenborg)

49

From Bastrup Lake to Strand-møllen by Øresund runs the 40 km long Mølleåe (Millstream). As the name depicts, the stream has been the driving force for many watermills ever since the Middle Ages. Among these is the former clothes factory's mill at Brede - now housing the National Museums third department. Here can be found the Danish Fishery Museum and the National Museum's educational exhibitions.

Canoes and rowing boats can be hired from Brede and other places.

(DSB: Lyngby)

Jægersborg Dyrehave (Deer Park). Each year, in November, the Hubertus Chase is held here as a tribute to the patron saint of hunting, Hubertus. The foremost rider acts as „fox" and leads the contestants over obstacles while the onlookers are amused by some of the horses which have their own interpretation of the route.

H.C. Andersen's City

The author of fairy tales, Hans Christian Andersen (1805 - 1875) is without doubt the most famous of the four world-famous beaux-esprits, thinkers and scientists who lived in Copenhagen during the 19th century. They were living at the same period through several decades; sometimes they would meet on the streets of Copenhagen and speake together, according to circumstances, on wind and weather or on deep spiritual, artistic or scientific affairs. On this page can be seen:

The philosopher Søren Kierkegaard (1813 - 1855), tremendous significance for existential thought.

The physicist Hans Christian Ørsted (1777 - 1851) tremendous significance for electrotechnics.

The priest and poet Nicolai Frederik Severin Grundtvig (1783-1872), tremendous significance for the enlightenment of the Danish people.

They did not all conform in 19th century Copenhagen. Hans Christian Andersen, whose behaviour was not considered to be normal in good society and intellectual circles, tells that on returning from one of his many foreign journeys, he heard the remark „*So, now he is home again, our world famous orangoutang!*"

Somewhat succinctly, the period from about 1800 to 1850 is called „Denmark's Golden Age". Nearly all aspects of spiritual life, all art forms and many branches of science blossomed in a way which astonishes posterity.

Søren Kierkegaard

Hans Christian Ørsted

N. F. S. Grundtvig

The reconstruction of the apartment Nyhavn 18, where H.C. Andersen lived for a number of years. (H.C. Andersen's House, Odense).

There is no natural explanation. The Golden Age, though, is often connected with the fact that the political-economic development through the 19th century was a series of catastrophes for Denmark and the capital. From the breakdown of the neutrality policy at the beginning of the century to Denmarks resounding defeat in the 2nd Schleswig war of 1864.

The houses in Nyhavn (New Harbour) look as they did when H.C. Andersen lived there. Once upon a time the old salts hung out here, and one can still get a tattoo. Today, most of the sailors come from the yachts that lie along the quay. There are amusing shops and a varied selection of restaurants and cafes; some are good eating places, others pay more attention to the music.

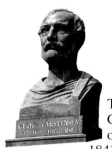

Tivoli in Copenhagen opened in 1843 on the former rampart territory. The initiator was Georg Carstensen. A newspaper wrote: *„Have you been to Tivoli? Isn't it charming; isn't it pleasant? For the past 14 days, every conversation in Copenhagen has begun with these words."* Another newspaper: *„It is a fairy garden"*. Tivoli was a success.

H.C. Andersen also visited Tivoli in 1843. But that was no success. The saucy singing girls in the cabaret caught sight of the celebrity and made fun of him. The shy, awkward man fled in panic.

Come! It is best to go in at the main entrance, half an hour before the performance begins at the Pantomime Theatre. Enjoy the music from the little pavillion on your right, while you wander along.

The large peacock which is the theatre's drop curtain, folds down. The performance begins. It is commedia dell' arte - here ballet and pantomime. Many of the dancers are from the Royal Ballet.
When the performance is over, the children begin to shout. It sounds like „Si no'et Pjerrot!" (Say something Pierrot!)

It is a reasonable request, as being a pantomime, not a word has been spoken during the performance. So Pierrot allows himself to be persuaded. He comes out in front of the curtain. Says something. Something or other. It always ends with the children as well as adults, enthusiastically shouting hurrah for something or other.

One continues to stroll, in a delightful frame of mind, further into the fairy garden.

(DSB: København H)

Si'
no'et
Pjerrot!

Churches

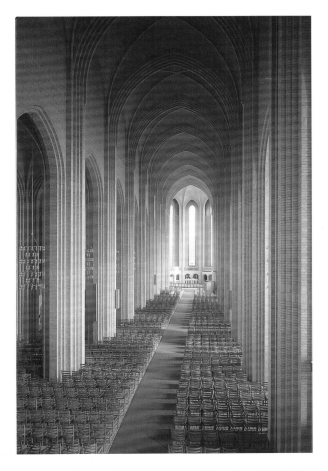

Although churches were built extensively in the 12th and 13th centuries - about 2,000 were erected all over the country - none of these are to be found in Copenhagen's inner city.

They have of course been there, but new churches have been built on their sites. Therefore the small, modest medieval buildings have disappeared into Renaissance, Baroque and Neo-classic style edifices with towers, spires and magnificent furniture and fittings.

Out in the suburbs, i.e. Brønshøj, Gentofte and Lyngby can be found the old type of church exemplifying the „typical Danish country church". It was this concept that P.V. Jensen Klint used as inspiration for the massive Grundtvig church, constructed at Bispebjerg in the years 1921-40.

All over, yellow hand-moulded bricks have been used for the walls; it was an honour for a brick-layer to be allowed to work here - only a handful were found to be skilled enough for the exacting work. The tower is 152 feet high, the nave 67 feet and about 2,000 people can be seated.

The great organ, built by Marcussen & Son in 1965 makes the church suitable for grand church concert arrangements.
On the opposite page can be seen one of the 32 feet high organ pipes.

(DSB: Emdrup)

In 1191, Absalon appointed one of his younger relatives, Peder Sunesen, as bishop of the diocese of Roskilde. He is named as founder of the Church of Our Lady in Copenhagen. No remains have been found, but it is known that the church burned down, probably for the fourth time, in July 1314. Shortly afterwards, in 1316, a church was built in best Gothic style, kindred to French cathedral Gothic as well as North German. Just about 150 years later, Christian I travelled to Rome and there obtained permission from the Pope to open a university in Copenhagen. It was built beside the Church of Our Lady and the University of Copenhagen was inaugurated with a big ceremony in the church.

Under the bombardment of the city by the English in September 1807, first the tower then the rest of the building burned down. Ten years later, Frederik VI laid the foundation stone for the altar in a new building. The Danish architect C.F. Hansen, who at that time was masterbuilder for rural buildings in Holsten, was chosen for the job. The famous Danish sculptor, Bertel Thorvaldsen was to decorate the church. His sculptures - Christ, the christening angel and the twelve apostles as well as several friezes and reliefs are in amazing harmony with the great room. Altogether it is a unique example of neo-classical building art.

(DSB: Nørreport)

One of the most characteristic towers to be seen over the roofs of Copenhagen is the one of „Vor Frelsers Kirke" - The Church of Our Saviour - with the outside spiral staircase leading to the top of the spire.

The church was built at the end of the 17th century in Dutch baroque style, designed by Lambert van Haven. The spire with its 150 steps, drawn by de Thurah, was raised in 1749-50.

„Frederikskirken's" (or „The Marble Church's") dome also makes its mark on Copenhagen's skyline. Frederik V laid the church's foundation stone in 1749. It was intended as a link in Eigtveds project „Frederiks city". On his death in 1754 the project was taken over by architect Jardin, but the construction was stopped in 1770. The unfinished building stood as a ruin until 1874 when C.F. Tietgen, financier and mæcenas, purchased it and commissioned architect I. Meldahl to complete the work.

St. Ansgar Church in Bredgade (1842) was designed by G.F. Hetsch. In 1941 it was inaugurated as the Roman Catholic Cathedral in Copenhagen.

Holmens Church was inaugurated in 1619 as the Navy's church. In the years previously, Christian IV had the former anchor-smithy converted for the purpose. Later, two trancepts were added and in 1705-8 a 59 meter long chapel was built on in the direction of the Stock Exchange moat. Tordenskjolds coffin, amongst others, lies here. A statue of the naval hero stands outside the church, made in 1868 by H.W. Bissen.

On Trinity Sunday, 1st June 1656, Trinity Church was inaugurated. The building work started in 1637, at the same time as the building of the Round Tower. Both were designed by Hans Steenwinkel the Younger and with Christian IV as entrepreneur. After the great fire in 1728, the church was rebuilt, almost unchanged. At its re-inauguration in 1731 the church obtained a new altarpiece and pulpit made by F. Ehbisch and the richly ornamented organ also originates from this year.

The English Church, St. Albans, stands in Churchill Park, close to Langelinie. It was built in the 1880s in English-Gothic style, designed by the English architect A.W. Bloomfield.

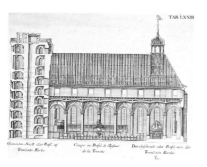

↖(DSB: Nørreport) ↑(DSB: Østerport)

The cathedral in Roskilde west of Copenhagen is the burial place for the Danish kings. The present church was founded in about 1170 by Bishop Absalon, and was completed about 1300. The towers were added during the 15th century. Since then the royal chapels have been added onto the north as well as the south side of the church. In 1636 Christian IV raised the slender copper spires on the towers.

In the cannons choir are two rows of choir stalls from 1420. Behind them is the large winged altarpiece, a Dutch carved piece from about 1560. According to tradition, it was to be sent to Gdansk, but when it passed Kronborg and Sound Dues had to be paid , it was valued very low and, as was their right, the custom officers bought the piece at the very low valuation price.

At the south side of the nave stands the organ from 1555. Opposite, is Christian IV's Chair, a rood loft sat up in 1610. The pulpit and font are also from that period.

Behind the altarpiece, in the choir, stands Queen Margrete I's marble sarcophagus. With very few exceptions, the whole of the Oldenborg royal line and four kings from the House of Glucksburg lie buried in Roskilde Cathedral.

(DSB: Roskilde)

Theatre & Music

↑(DSB: Nørreport) ↓(DSB: Svanemøllen)

The Boat Theatre stage their performances in a converted barge, purchased in 1972 for the purpose. For the first years, the performances were mostly for children, but in 1980, with Holberg's „Ulysses von Ithacia", also for adults. The following year, the Boat Theatre obtained its present berth in Nyhavn where it is an important part of the milieu.

On 18th December 1748 the first Royal Theatre opened on Kongens Nytorv. The present, larger theatre, designed by J.V. Dahlerup and built on the same spot was inaugurated in 1874. During the past 250 years, the most important works from Danish as well as international drama, ballet and opera have been performed here. From 1931 the theatre has also had at its disposal the „New Scene" also called „The Nesting Box". The theatre has also in later years used different localities for intimate and experimental theatre.

In the large gasometer at Østerbro - Østre Gasværk (East Gasworks) - there has been shown over the past ten years a selection of largely musical shows ranging from small closet plays designed for the place, to large foreign musicals, as for example, „Les Miserables".
The picture opposite is from the Danish musical „Atlantis" for which Østre Gasværk has supplied the physical setting for a big success which has resulted in considerable international interest.

The Broadcasting House on Rosenørns Allé, designed by Vilh. Lauritzen was completed in 1938. The concert hall was fitted out a few years later, but because of the German occupation, its inauguration was celebrated after May 1945. Countless famous Danish and foreign conductors and soloists, together with the almost 100 members of the Radio Symphony Orchestra and Radio Choir, have performed international classical music works of composers from the earliest Renaissance to Karlheinz Stockhausen.

↑(DSB: Nørreport)   ↓(DSB: Vesterport)

Since the middle of the 1930s, a lot of good jazz music has been played here in Denmark. Several excellent musicians have carved out a career for themselves both here and abroad, and innumerable gramophone and CD recordings have helped to make jazz a part of our musical life. A recurring annual Summer event is the Copenhagen Jazz Festival, where music is played outdoors, indoors, different places around town and at all hours of the day and night.

All year round, one often stops to listen when walking on the streets in the city. Young music students take up a stand and play so that it is a real pleasure - and get a much needed supplement to their study allowance.

At Dyrehavsbakken at Klampenborg one can also find music-making. The most famous and best-loved establishment is „Bakkens Hvile" where many of our best ballad singers have begun their career. Otherwise, it is mostly dance music which is sought after here.

Danish cuisine

On the left hand plate lies the meat from the soup, and, if it is absolutely correct, two or three types of sausage. Beer? Yes. Snaps? Absolutely. If you keep to tradition, the meal finishes with „æbleskiver" (battercakes) with blackcurrant rum.

Brown cabbage with bacon. Roast pork with crackling - and red cabbage. Boiled, smoked ham with sugar potatoes and creamed kale. In general, different sorts of cabbage supplemented with every possible type of pork.

Denmark is surrounded by the sea and Danes eat a lot of fish. Preparation is often extremely simple. For example, boiled cod with good, boiled potatoes, grated horseradish, chopped hard-boiled egg and piping hot butter sauce.

Danish cuisine is influenced by the fact that not so very long ago, the country had agriculture as its main industry - and that our climate in the winter is rather harsh.

That meant the use of good raw materials, a tradition which happily has been maintained, and some rather heavy dishes. One of these, Yellow Pea Soup, manages to split the nation in two halves. One that hates it and one that loves it. It is seldom that one sees it on a restaurant menu, though in some places it is served on a certain day of the week.

Then the restaurant is filled with a faithful congregation that reverently regards the two plates which are requisite.

On the right, the one with the most delightful, strong soup. Of yellow dried peas, carrots, celery, parsnip, root parsley leeks, small onions and thyme, all cooked with fresh and smoked and salt pork.

The new Danish kitchen - especially in restaurants - has taken so much inspiration from particularly the French, that one can no longer actually talk of a national identity.

...med det grønne

...BRØDSSEDDEL

		Rugb.	Franskbr.

Spiced herring

...sild ....

....m/rejer ....ulade ....

...ejer m/citron og mayonnai...

8. Gravad laks på surbrød ......

9. »**FROKOST I DET GRØNNE**«
Lille anretning m/sild, lun leverpos...
roastbeef, kartoffelsalat, ost, brød ...

Se i øvrigt vor tavle ....

*Eel and
scrambled
egg*

10. Mørbradbøf m/løg og cha...
11. Ribbensteg m/rød...
12. Roastbeef...
13. R...

22. ...
23. ...
24. Gammel ost m/fedt og sky (på surb.) ...
25. Gorgonzola m/løg og æg .....
26. Mild ost ....

....ert frites m/syltetøj ...

*The Vet's Midnight
snack*

*Danish strawberries taste
better than those
cultivated in a warmer
climate*

On the other hand, open sandwiches are our national pride. In its origins it is a piece of bread with a scraping of butter and laid on top a piece of cold meat, sausage, cheese, or something similar. Most Danes eat their daily lunch like that.

However, in restaurants it has been further developed. Every piece has to be a work of art. When it has been created by a master, not only does it look good, but the different ingredients are matched so that they suit each other and enhance the taste.

A good „smørrebrød" tip is to visit one of the many small luncheon restaurants that lie off the main streets, for instance in the side streets off „Strøget", on Vester Voldgade, Frederiksholm-kanal and Gl. Torv. They are often found in a basement and do not go in for smart decorations.

The clientele is very varied. Artisans; business people; journalists from the nearby newspaper offices; politicians. It is always possible that the gentleman you see, deep in thought, with a pencil in his hand and a list in front of him, is our Prime Minister.

The said list is a „smørrebrød" menu. It is possible to order one's smørrebrød unspecified, but if you land in a place where one can only order unspeci-fied, hurry up and leave again. You have come to the wrong place.

Therefore, ask for the smørrebrød list. It is that business's patent of nobility, as no two restaurants have the same. There is one space to mark if you want ryebread, another for whitebread.

Start with herring. There ought to be five or six different ones to choose from. In season, there is smoked herring which is delicious and quite different from the other herring suggestions. Put a cross for ryebread, of course. A piece with hand-peeled fjord shrimps? (Whitebread). They are tiny and a Danish speciality. Very delicious and very expensive. A piece with eel? A „vet's midnight snack"?

Finish off with cheese. There are many fine Danish cheeses. Put a cross for whitebread, unless you have chosen one of the really mature cheeses. (In some places you get a drop of rum on these). In which case it should be ryebread.

When you have filled in your list, you deliver it and wait.

A quarter of an hour will pass before the smørre-brød arrives. It is not lying ready-made, but is freshly composed for each order.

One drinks beer with smørrebrød and a snaps with the herring. There are many kinds. Red Ålborg is the most „snapslike" - flavoured with caraway and rough. A milder one, for example, is Brøndum. Incidentally, many believe a snaps should also be enjoyed with the cheese.

C.W. Eckersberg: Woman in front of a mirror (1841)

↑**The National Museum** lies in the centre of Copenhagen, close to the Town Hall Square. It is Denmark's largest - a central museum which illustrates the nation's history from ancient to modern times. An extensive modernisation which was carried out in 1989-92 has made it even more absorbing.

For those who seek more beauty, knowledge or an interesting experience, there are various possibilities in the city and suburbs: Museums like pearls on a string. Some of them are shown on the following pages.

Arbejdermuseet

Rømersgade 22, DK-1362 København K (DSB: Nørreport)

Permanent exhibition: The industrial workers life from the close of the 19th century until the 1950s.

A kitchen in hard times - an appartment from the 1930s

Karen Blixen Museet

Rungsted Strandvej 111, DK-2960 Rungsted Kyst
(DSB: Rungsted Kyst)

Karen Blixen (1885-1962) was born hereat Rungstedlund and wrote most of her books here. The museum consists of the authoress's home, an exhibition, bookshop and cafe.

Ewalds Room

Davids Samling

Kronprinsessegade 30, DK-1306 København K (DSB: Nørreport)

Northern Europe's largest collection of Islamic art from about the 8th to the 19th century. Also European art, mostly 18th century.

A miniature from India: „Lovers in a landscape" (ca. 1775)

Eksperimentariet®

Tuborg Havnevej 7, DK-2900 Hellerup
(DSB: Hellerup)

Over 300 activities and changing special exhibitions which make it fun to learn more about nature, technology and yourself.

Pilot demonstration

Frihedsmuseet

Churchillparken, DK-1263 København K

(DSB: Østerport)

The main museum covering the period of occupation. It describes developments from 1940-45 with most emphasis on the Resistance. Records and collection of photographs.

Frilandsmuseet Sorgenfri

Kongevejen 100 & I.C. Modewegsvej, DK-2800 Lyngby (DSB: Sorgenfri)

45 old farmhouses and other rural buildings from Denmark, the Farøe Islands, South Schleswig, Scania, Halland and Småland have been built on the museum's 36 hectare large area. Illustrates life in the country from 1700-1900.

Glyptoteket

Dantes Plads 7, DK-1556 København V (DSB: København H)

New Carlsberg Glypothek shows large collections of Egyptian, Greek, Roman and Etruscan art, fine examples from French artists and sculptors as well as paintings from the Danish Golden Age. A large winter garden with modern sculptures.

Guiness World of Records Museum

Østergade 16, DK-1100 København K (DSB: Nørreport)

The worlds most thrilling records presented in vital and exciting surroundings. Dive down under the sea, experience the conquest of the universe and visit the worlds of music, sport and film.
15 different themes.

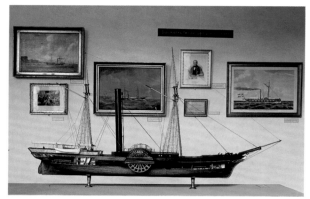

Handels- og Søfartsmuseet

Kronborg, DK-3000 Helsingør (DSB: Helsingør)

Denmark's largest maritime museum. Danish shipping and trade from about 1400, including shipbuilding, navigation, navigation in Greenland waters, trade in the colonies and modern container transport.

Open model of the paddle steamer „Iris"

Den Hirschsprungske Samling

Stockholmsgade 20, DK-2100 København Ø (DSB: Østerport)

An exceptional collection of Danish art from the 19th and beginning of the 20th century. Works of amongst others, the Golden Age painters Eckersberg and Købke, the Skagen painters Michael and Anna Ancher and P.S. Krøyer. In addition, Philipsen, Hammershøi, artists from Funen and Danish symbolists.

C.W. Eckersberg; Woman in front of a mirror (1841)

Jagt- og Skovbrugsmuseet

Folehavevej 15 - 17, DK-2970 Hørsholm (DSB: Rungsted Kyst)

One of the largest of its kind in Europe. The history of Danish forestry from about 1850 to 1950. A collection of game, traps, hunting weapons and accessories that illustrate hunting in Denmark since the last ice-age.

Crossbow

Kunstindustrimuseet

Bredgade 68, DK-1260 København K (DSB: Østerport)

The collections consist of handicrafts and design from the Middle Ages to modern times as well as Chinese and Japanese art through the ages.
The library is the main reference library in the field.

Hans J. Wegner: China-chair No.4 (1945)

Københavns Bymuseum

Vesterbrogade 59, DK-1620 København V

(DSB: København H)

Concerns the development of the city, its culture and history. Illustrates life in Copenhagen through the ages. A minor exhibition of the philosopher Søren Kierkegaard. There is an adjacent museum street with old fittings.

Model of Copenhagen about 1530

Louisiana

Museum of Modern Art
Gl. Strandvej 13, DK-3050
Humlebæk (DSB: Humlebæk)

With a large number of exhibitions of usually modern art, it is firmly established in the art world. The large park gives ideal surroundings for the enjoyment of sculpture while indoors is found a collection of the works of the 20th century's most important artists.

A permanent exhibition of the works of the „Cobra" painters.

Medicinsk-Historisk Museum

Bredgade 62, DK-1260 København K (DSB: Østerport)

The exhibition shows the development of Danish medical science through the ages.

Dentist's surgery from 1885

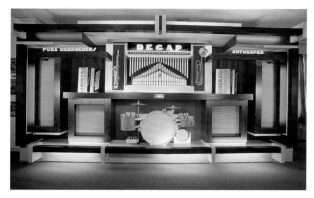

Mekanisk Musik Museum

Rungstedvej 1C, DK-2970 Hørsholm
(DSB: Rungsted Kyst)
Unique collection of fairground organs, mechanical pianos, automatic violins, musical boxes, automatic orchestras, barrel organs, phonographs, etc. Non-stop tours.

Bacigalupo Barrel Organ

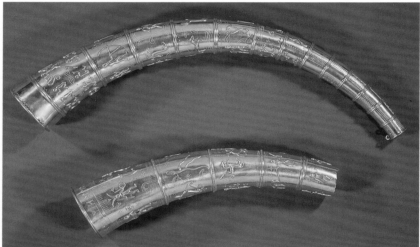

The Sun Carriage and The Gildenhorns

Nationalmuseet

Frederiksholms Kanal 12, DK-1220 København K (DSB: København H)
Denmarks main cultural historical museum with collections that illustrate the history of the nation all through the ages. There is also an ethnographic exhibition, the Royal Mint and Medal collection and Antique collection.

Nivaagaards Malerisamling

Gammel Strandvej 2, DK-2990 Nivå (DSB: Nivå)

An exquisite collection of European art from the 16th and 17th centuries including a female portrait by Rembrandt and a landscape by Claude Lorrain. Besides, a fine collection of Danish art, mostly from the Golden Age. Concurrent special exhibitions in a part of the museum.

L.A. Ring: Lundbye's bench by Arre lake

Ordrupgaardsamlingen

Vilvordevej 110, DK-2920 Charlottenlund

(DSB: Ordrup/Klampenborg)

A distinguished collection of French and Danish art from the 19th and 20th century. Outstanding paintings by Danish artists and masterpieces by French artists such as Delacroix, Corot, Courbet, Manet, Degas, Renoir, Pissarro, Sisley, Monet, Cézanne, Gauguin and Matisse.

Johan Thomas Lundbye: Winter landscape (1841)

Orlogsmuseet

Overgaden oven Vandet 58, DK-1415 København K (DSB: København H)

Shows historical naval collections that consist of the Navy's ship models from 1600 to modern times as well as weapons and artillery, shipbuilding, uniforms, ships equipment and maritime art.

The command bridge in the submarine „Spækhuggeren"

Planetarium, Tycho Brahe

Gammel Kongevej 10, DK-1610 København V (DSB: Vesterport)

A performance every hour starting at 11 a.m. Experience the star-studded night sky as it can be seen from dark, empty places, or the special omnimax films on astronomy, space and the wilderness, where picture and sound carry the spectator into the heart of events.

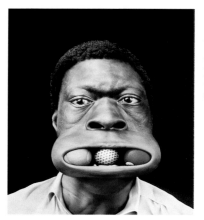

Ripley's Believe It or Not!

Rådhuspladsen 57, DK-1550 København V (DSB: København H)

Robert L. Ripley - artist, journalist and explorer, during his adventurous life sought out unusual objects. Here, his incredible collection of oddities is exhibited.

Rosenborg Slot

De Danske Kongers kronologiske Samling - Øster Voldgade 4A
DK-1350 København K
(DSB: Nørreport)

The museum is from 1833. The interiors from about 1610 to 1860 with collections of silver, glass, porcelain (Flora Danica), ivory and costumes. In the Treasury are royal crowns, regalia, the crown jewels, etc.

The Green Cabinet

Statens Museum for kunst

Sølvgade 48 - 50, DK-1307 København K (DSB: Østerport)

Denmark's National Gallery. Rich collections of European and Danish paintings and sculptures from the 17th century until now. Emphasis on Danish Golden Age art. Large Nolde collection. Changing exhibitions of Danish and international art.

Storm P. - Museet

Frederiksberg Runddel, DK-2000 Frederiksberg
(DSB: Frederiksberg)
An exhibition of the Danish humorist Robert Storm Petersen's drawings and paintings that span the social critical satires from his young days to his later years humorous newspaper cartoons. Also his study and large collection of pipes.

Storm P.: Tightrope. From cradle to grave (ca.1945)

Thorvaldsens Museum

Porthusgade 2, DK-1213 København K
(DSB: København H)
Bertel Thorvaldsen (1770-1844) - his sculptures with drawn and modelled sketches for these. Also his collections of antique objects and paintings executed by contemporary European and Danish artists.

1st Floor, South corridor

Tøjhusmuseet

Tøjhusgade 3, DK-1214 København K
(DSB: København H)
The museum's permanent exhibition shows the development of weaponry from the invention of gunpowder to the present day. The exhibition is housed in Christian IV's armoury built 1598-1604. Usually there are one or more special exhibitions.

Model of „Trinity", Christian IV's flagship

Interiors from exhibition halls

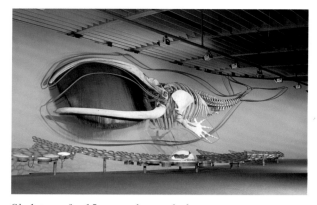

Skeleton of a 15 metre long whale

Vikingeskibshallen

Strandengen, DK-4000 Roskilde (DSB: Roskilde)

Contains 5 viking ships: 2 trading vessels, 2 warships and a smaller vessel from about the year 1000. They were all found in and raised from Roskilde Fjord. There are full scale copies that sail with guests on the fjord.

Zoologisk Museum

Universitetsparken 15, DK-2100 København Ø (DSB: Nørrebro)

The collections cover all categories of the animal kingdom on the planet.
Exhibitions: „Denmarks Animal Kingdom" and „From Pole to Pole". Also, in the Ocean Hall, animal life in the seas from whales to small creatures on the sea-floor.

Bertel Thorvaldsen (1770 - 1844); Ganymed with Jupiter's eagle. Marble.

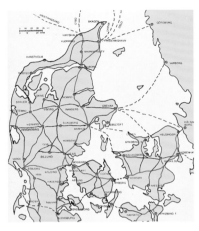

Denmark is a member of EU, UN, NATO and the Nordic Council. The Danish state church is Lutheran-evangelical. Denmark has 5,196,000 inhabitants of whom 1,346,00 live in the city of Copenhagen. Out of Denmark's 43,100 km2, the peninsular Jutland takes up 29,800 km2 and the 306 islands - of which 83 are inhabited - 13,300 km2. The total coastline is 7,310 km. The Farøe Islands and Greenland also belong to the Kingdom of Denmark, though now they are autonomous.

Currency: Danish crowns (DKK), 1 crown = 100 øre. Denmark has a temperate coastal climate. The hottest month is July, the coldest, January. Cloud cover is least in May and greatest in December. May and June have the most sunshine, December the least sunshine. The lowest temperature measured in Denmark is -31 degrees, the highest measured, 36 degrees.

From Denmark there are direct connections by ferry to Poland, Norway, Sweden and Bornholm. From Copenhagen's main station there are train connections to the most of Europe and with the InterCity train (IC3), one can travel fast and comfortably to the larger towns in Denmark. Copenhagen's Airport is the main airport for Scandinavia and the South-Baltic region. It is very modern and well equipped. Technically, the airport is one of the most advanced.

ISBN: 87-87108-40-2 © 1996 GRØNLUND'S

Text: Grønlund's & Jesper Vang Hansen
Translated by: Vivian Hovmand

Photo: Rigmor Mydtskov, Jørgen Grønlund, Christian Erichsen,
Nikolaj Meding, Carsten Andreasen, Peter Grønlund, Lone Kjæhr,
Kim Wichmann, Royal Copenhagen, Lindberg press, Allan Schnipper,
Ole Woldbye, Lars Grunwald, Jens Frederiksen, Geert Brovad,
Louis Schnakenburg and Biofoto.

GRØNLUND'S FORLAG
Svanevang 4 - DK-3450 Allerød - E-mail: gronlund@inet.zitech.dk